Franklin Delano Roosevelt

![Cherry Lake Press logo] CHERRY LAKE PRESS

Published in the United States of America by Cherry Lake Publishing Group
Ann Arbor, Michigan
www.cherrylakepublishing.com

Reading Adviser: Beth Walker Gambro, MS, Ed., Reading Consultant, Yorkville, IL
Book Designer: Jennifer Wahi
Illustrator: Jeff Bane

Photo Credits: © Spiroview Inc/Shutterstock, 5; National Portrait Gallery, Smithsonian Institution, gift of Francis A. DiMauro, 7; Margaret DeM. Brown/Library of Congress, 9; Harris & Ewing/Library of Congress, 11, 17; Architect of the Capitol, 13; Mitchell Loeb/DeGolyer Library, Southern Methodist University, 19; FDR Presidential Library & Museum, Gift of Beatrice Perskie Foxman and Dr. Stanley B. Foxman via Wikimedia Commons (CC BY 2.0), 21

Cherry Lake Press is an imprint of Cherry Lake Publishing Group.

Library of Congress Cataloging-in-Publication Data

Names: Trockman, Ben, author. | Bane, Jeff, 1967- illustrator.
Title: Franklin Delano Roosevelt / written by Ben Trockman ; [illustrated by Jeff Bane].
Description: Ann Arbor, Michigan : Cherry Lake Publishing, 2023. | Series: My itty-bitty bio | Audience: Grades K-1 | Summary: "Explore the life of former president Franklin Delano Roosevelt in a simple, age-appropriate way that helps young readers develop word recognition and reading skills. Developed in partnership with Easterseals and written by a member of the disability community, this title helps all readers learn from those who make a difference in our world. The My Itty-Bitty Bio series celebrates diversity, inclusion, and the values that readers of all ages can aspire to"-- Provided by publisher.
Identifiers: LCCN 2023009118 | ISBN 9781668927243 (hardcover) | ISBN 9781668928295 (paperback) | ISBN 9781668929766 (ebook) | ISBN 9781668931240 (pdf)
Subjects: LCSH: Roosevelt, Franklin D. (Franklin Delano), 1882-1945--Juvenile literature. | Presidents--United States--Biography--Juvenile literature. | People with disabilities--United States--Biography--Juvenile literature.
Classification: LCC E807 .T745 2023 | DDC 973.917092 [B]--dc23/eng/20230313
LC record available at https://lccn.loc.gov/2023009118

Printed in the United States of America
Corporate Graphics

table of contents

About the author: When he's not writing, making jokes, or public speaking, Ben Trockman works in the communications industry. Ben also serves as a city councilman in his hometown of Evansville, Indiana.

About the illustrator: Jeff Bane and his two business partners own a studio along the American River in Folsom, California, home of the 1849 Gold Rush. When Jeff's not sketching or illustrating for clients, he's either swimming or kayaking in the river to relax.

About our partnership: This title was developed in partnership with Easterseals to support its mission of empowering people with disabilities. Through their national network of affiliates, Easterseals provides essential services and on-the-ground supports to more than 1.5 million people each year.

I am Franklin Delano Roosevelt.
People call me FDR.

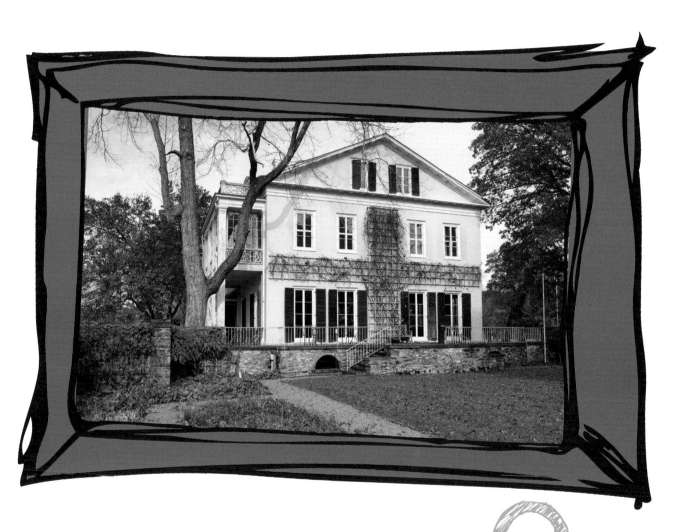

Do you have a nickname?

I was a New York state senator.
Then I got **polio**. I was very sick.
I couldn't use my legs.

I worked hard. I got stronger.
I used a wheelchair. I became
New York's governor.

Theodore Roosevelt was my hero. He was a U.S. president. He was my cousin.

Who is your hero?

I ran for president in 1932. I became the 32nd U.S. president.

13

I was the first president to fly on a plane. I had a dog named Fala. We went everywhere together.

What's your favorite animal?

America was in the **Great Depression**. People lost their jobs. I made a plan. I called it the New Deal. I explained it over the radio.

I was elected president four times. That is more than anyone else in history. I died in 1945. I was still president.

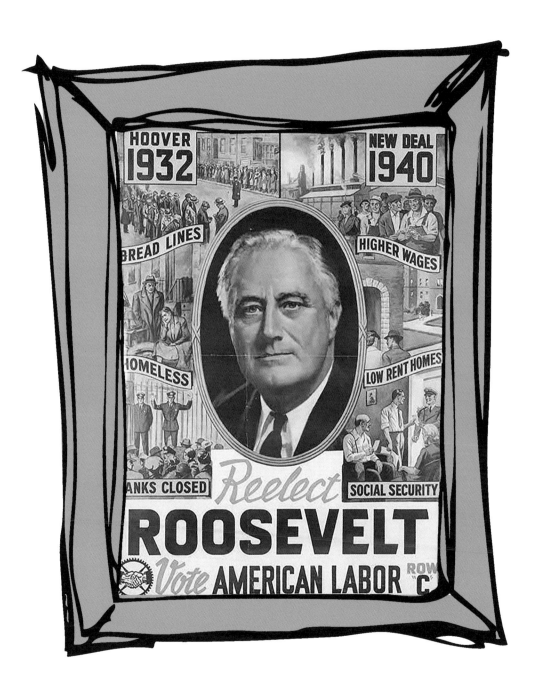

My **legacy** lives on. My story inspires people. Being disabled did not stop me.

What would you like to ask me?

1921

1880

↑
Born
1882

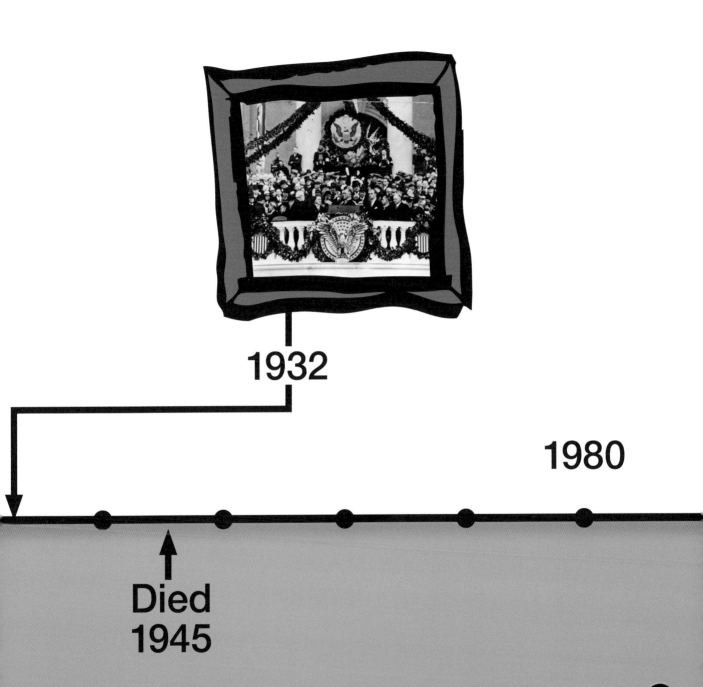

1932

1980

Died
1945

glossary

Great Depression (GRAYT deh-PRESH-uhn) period of U.S. history from 1929 to 1941 where people were out of work and had very little money

legacy (LEH-guh-see) something handed down from one generation to another

polio (POHL-ee-oh) a virus that spreads and can affect a person's spinal cord, causing paralysis

index